FIND YOUR PERFECT JOB

THE INSIDE GUIDE FOR
YOUNG PROFESSIONALS

SCOTT SMITH

First Edition

ISBN 978-0-9843938-0-0

Printed in the United States of America.

Published by Career Strategies Media.

www.PerfectJobBook.com

CONTENTS

PREFACE:

MY STORY

Graduating from a prestigious liberal arts college, I had many career options before me. A lot of careers sounded exciting, but which was the best fit for me? It was a big decision, and I was concerned that if I made the wrong choice, it would be very difficult to change careers later on. Some career options required graduate school first, and this raised the stakes even higher. What if I invested the time and money to get a graduate degree only to find out once I was in a full-time job afterward that I hadn't pursued the right career?

I tried to weigh the pros and cons of the different career options, but that didn't get me very far. You see, not having experienced even one full-time professional job yet, I didn't, and couldn't, know the right questions to ask myself in order to determine what job would be the best fit for me. Similarly, I considered both business school and law school, but, as an outsider, there was a limit to how well I could understand what those programs were really like. So, like most young professionals in their 20s, I plodded forward, trying different careers, and learning through firsthand experience what the real world of professional jobs and graduate schools was like.

Below is a chronological list of all the full-time jobs I have held since college (including "contract" jobs and summer positions held during graduate school). I found success at each step, but it wasn't until my last stop that I landed my Perfect Job.

- o Associate marketing specialist for a computer manufacturer
- o Commercial credit analyst for a regional bank
- o Telecommunications regulatory attorney for the Federal Communications Commission in Washington, D.C.
- o Entertainment lawyer for a major motion picture studio in Hollywood, California
- o Teaching assistant (acting professor) at a major university (part-time)
- o Corporate IT trainer for a Fortune 500 company
- o Banking/mergers & acquisitions attorney for one of the largest law firms in the country
- o Telecommunications transactions attorney for one of Boston's largest corporations
- o Intellectual property/technology attorney for a Silicon Valley law firm
- o Assistant general counsel for an industrial manufacturer
- o Investment banker on Wall Street
- o Equity research analyst for an investment management firm

I completed several rounds of grad school applications during this time. This included taking the following standardized admissions exams:

- o LSAT (for law school)

- o GMAT (for business school)
- o GRE (for most other graduate school programs)

I completed the following professional graduate programs and licensures:

- o Juris doctor from a top 20 law school
- o Massachusetts and California bar licenses
- o Master of business administration from arguably the world's top business school

I researched many different career options throughout these 17 years after college and conducted more than 300 informational interviews. (An informational interview involves contacting people you may or may not know, but who work in careers in which you are interested, and then meeting with them to gain insight into their careers and how they conducted their job search.) I participated in more than 300 actual job interviews. Along the way, I had countless conversations with other young professionals and graduate school students, comparing experiences and things we were learning firsthand about careers and grad school programs.

When I finally arrived at my Perfect Job, I felt that I had learned all of the criteria one needs to know in order to define his or her ideal job. These were the questions and answers I didn't know when my career journey began after college. I also had learned numerous successful strategies for landing hard-to-get jobs, including resume, cover letter, interview, and networking tips and techniques. In addition, I had gained an insider's knowledge of law school and the legal profession, as well as of business school. My cumulative perspective on these two programs was fairly unique, having attended both programs full time and separately from one another at different leading universities.

From my conversations with my peers, it was clear that most young professionals faced the same hurdles I did in finding the careers that fit them best and making the important decisions about graduate schools. As my own journey progressed, I found myself more and more advising others about *their* career searches. I was sharing with them the criteria I had learned in order to define one's Perfect Job as well as other crucial career and grad school considerations. I realized I could help a lot more people by writing a book, so I took everything I had learned and created an easy-to-use career guide for all young professionals. This is the book you now hold in your hands, *Find Your Perfect Job: The Inside Guide for Young Professionals.*

The goal of this book is to give young professionals direction and focus in finding and landing the job that is best for them. My experiences taught me an immense amount about different careers, job-search strategies, and graduate school programs. I have captured all my personal experience and knowledge and summarized it in this multipurpose career guidebook. In essence, I wrote the career book I wish I'd had during all my prior job searches. **By sharing with you everything I learned, I want to help you make the best possible decisions at each critical juncture of your own career search.** I hope you enjoy reading this book, and that it helps you achieve your dreams. Good luck in finding your Perfect Job!

CHAPTER 1

INTRODUCTION

How This Job-Search Book Is Different

This book is unlike any other job-search or career book available. First and foremost, it is written by someone whose professional and academic experiences and successes are broad and deep. (My full background is detailed in the Preface.) I have spent more time in my 20s and 30s undertaking job searches and career research, working in a range of careers, and completing professional graduate degrees than probably any other person you will find—certainly more than any other job-search/career book author. In fact, most of those other authors are career counselors with little actual real-world professional experience of their own! Everything in *this* book is based on my firsthand experience and complemented by numerous informational interviews with successful professionals and conversations with accomplished peers. **This book gives you the unfiltered inside scoop on job searching, the corporate world, law school, and business school.**

Most job-search-book authors also are not young professionals themselves. Unlike the books they write, this book was written by your peer, someone who has gone through and therefore can personally relate to the career issues that you as a young professional face. ***Find Your Perfect Job*** **was written by a successful young professional in order to help other young professionals achieve their dreams.** Most job-search books are for general audiences, whereas this book is specifically tailored for young professionals. (That being said, much of the information in this book will help people of any age.)

You probably have already noticed another way this book is different from most—it's short. Most job-search books are LONG. I believe those serve as a security blanket for the reader. He or she reasons: "Well, since this book is *so* big, it must have *lots* of good ideas for me." Yet how many of those books actually get read cover to cover? Not many! Those books are too broad and verbose, and they lose focus. Reading them is like studying for an academic course, using an unwieldy, boring textbook. Even if you wade through all the superfluous information to get to the few nuggets of truth inside those books, that wastes a lot of your time—precious time you could have used instead to look for a job. This book focuses on the essential information you need to identify and land your Perfect Job. ***Find Your Perfect Job* is concise and straightforward, and thus easier and quicker to read and put to use than the other job-search books out there.**

Many books only address one or two parts of the job-search process, such as resume writing. **This book is a complete guide—a one-stop shop covering *all* the major parts of a job search.** Learn how to choose the best career; what the important resume, cover letter, interview, and networking skills are; how to break into a new career; what you should do on your first day on your job; and much more! Plus, there is an in-depth analysis of business school and law school for those interested in those programs.

Finally, unlike many books, *Find Your Perfect Job* targets your *ideal* job. Let's be honest—job searching stinks. It's even more painful when the economy is in a recession, because fewer opportunities are available. Yet there's no way around doing a job search, unless you don't need a job for some reason. (If that's the case, then, um, thanks for buying my book anyway!) So, if you are going to endure the trials and tribulations of a job search, you might as well pursue the *best* job for you—your Perfect Job. This book's strategy of identifying and landing your Perfect Job also helps you avoid doing another job search later on (i.e., it saves you from pursuing the wrong job and then undertaking a second job search to switch into the right job). ***Find Your Perfect Job* sets the highest of goals: matching you to your Perfect Job and helping you land it, showing you how to do both in the smartest and most direct way possible.**

The Heart of the Book

The heart of this book is what I call the "Perfect Job Profile." This is a framework, or road map, to define your Perfect Job. It contains a series of questions, the answers to which together will identify your Perfect Job. Think of the Perfect Job Profile as a system to organize the things you already know about yourself and the insights you learn along the way in your quest for your ideal job. Your Perfect Job Profile will give you direction and focus, the fundamental basis from which to build a successful job search.

What "Perfect Job" Means

What's your "Perfect Job?" It is the job that makes you happiest, that you gain fulfillment from doing, that you actually enjoy, and that you look forward to going to each day. Of course, it's important to remember that this is *work*, not *fun*. But there is no reason work cannot be as close to what you would consider fun as possible. Most successful people I know tell me that they either love their jobs or enjoy what they are doing. People who do the job that is "perfect" for them are naturally the most likely to succeed, providing them with even more satisfaction.

Although no job is perfect in the literal sense of the word, *Find Your Perfect Job* will guide you toward the job that is as close to perfect as possible. There might be more than one close-to-perfect job for you, but to keep things simple and increase your chances of professional happiness and success, this book will guide you to the one job that is closest to perfect.

How This Book Works—An Overview

This book provides you with a simple process to find your Perfect Job:

Define Your Perfect Job

Chapter 2 of this book presents a straightforward framework for you to use to identify your Perfect Job. You will answer a series of insightful questions that focus you on the specific characteristics of your Perfect Job. You will record your answers and together those answers will represent the Profile of your Perfect Job. Next, you will identify a real job title and employers that match your Perfect Job Profile.

Although I would caution against putting too much pressure on yourself to try to figure everything out early on, it will only help your career journey if you start off in the right direction through knowing as many specifics as possible of what your Perfect Job will look like. This is true whether your Perfect Job is an immediate possibility or one you work toward down the road.

Chapter 3 features additional considerations and challenges you may encounter in choosing and pursuing your Perfect Job. Several topics are addressed, including the importance of internships and ways to handle the graduate school decision.

Land Your Perfect Job

Chapter 4 of this book details successful strategies to receive an offer letter for the Perfect Job you identified in your Perfect Job Profile. Resume, cover letter, and interview secrets are revealed, and techniques are provided for overcoming prior-work-experience requirements when you have no direct experience.

A bad economy can be an additional hurdle for you in your quest for your Perfect Job. The strategies in this chapter are devised to help overcome difficult economic times, including specific advice on networking and getting around human resources "gatekeepers."

Business School and Law School

Chapter 5 of this book is for those of you who are considering either of the two main professional programs in the U.S.: business school and law school. These programs are tremendous commitments of time, money, and effort, but they may be worth it if they provide you with the training and contacts needed to land your Perfect Job. Because I attended both business school and law school full time and separately from one another, I present a unique firsthand perspective in comparing the two. At the end of this chapter, I discuss some popular career opportunities for business school students.

Chapter 6 targets the legal profession and debunks the myths about law school and being a lawyer. There are a lot of misconceptions out there, and you need to know what you are getting into before undertaking three years of law school to become a lawyer.

Final Advice

Chapter 7 wraps up the book and provides some pointers for success when you start your Perfect Job.

Now let's get you that Perfect Job, ASAP!

CHAPTER 2

DEFINE YOUR PERFECT JOB

Time to Dream

First, a motivational message: Go for it! You only live once! You are going to spend many more hours of your life at work than anywhere else, so why not find the best job for you, your Perfect Job? No regrets, no looking back, no "what if"s. Believe in yourself, and let's get started!

Spend Time Now, Save Trouble Later

Take the time to complete your Perfect Job Profile *before* accepting a job somewhere. Don't treat your job search as trial and error. It takes too much work to land a good job; don't waste that effort by taking an opportunity that isn't fully thought through. Plus, if you keep trying different jobs in trial-and-error fashion, you harm your employability because prospective employers will see you as a job-hopper who never commits. I cannot stress this next point enough: Put additional time in *now* to do your job search right, and you will *save* time in the long run by avoiding the need for multiple job searches. You also will avoid the angst that goes along with being in the wrong job and with changing jobs too.

I needed to change jobs several times before I got to my Perfect Job—it was a lot of work! Take what I learned through years of research and experience to land your Perfect Job more quickly and directly.

What Makes Up Your Perfect Job

Your Perfect Job is not simply the specific activities that you perform for an employer. Whom you work with (bosses, coworkers, clients) and where you work (type of company, geographic location) can be just as important in defining your Perfect Job as what your actual job responsibilities are. Your Perfect Job is the entire collection of factors that are important to you. Your Perfect Job Profile is a detailed list of all of these factors, and the synergies between them.

It is unlikely that you land a job right away that hits every single one of the factors you list in your Profile. However, you still need to define your ideal job at the earliest possible time, because it will give you direction and will help you evaluate opportunities as they come. Use your Perfect Job Profile to judge how close an opportunity is to your ideal and how important the things that are missing are to you. In this way you will be able to make the best decisions for yourself at each step of your career journey.

Instructions for Creating Your Perfect Job Profile

The next section lists all of the job factors you need to consider in order to define your Perfect Job. The factors are presented as questions, and they are listed in order of importance. **Take out an 8½" x 11" piece of paper and write down your answers to every question (or open an electronic document representing a single page to do this). Write the topic of each of the ten questions, followed by your answer.** For any factor you feel is particularly important to you in defining your Perfect Job, add a star next to it. Try to fit all of your notes on one side of a page, if possible. This will force you to be concise and to record only the most important information.

You may not know the answers yet for some of the questions. Do your best to record an answer, but if you can't, then write "to be determined" after the factor on your Profile. **Your Perfect Job Profile is a "living" document that will evolve over time. Edit it as you learn more about yourself and your preferences, making it more complete and precise.**

Some questions are presented as either/or, in order to force you to make a choice and thereby get a direction. However, it is possible that you will be open to several or even all of the choices. If this is the case, then record the combination of choices. Just be sure to be as specific as possible, and wherever you can make a choice or at least exclude one or more of the options, do so.

(Note: The word "company" is used in this section and throughout the book for simplicity's sake. It is meant to include all types of organizations that could employ you, including for-profit businesses, hospitals, schools, not-for-profit organizations, government offices, etc.)

Create Your Perfect Job Profile

Answer all of these questions to create the Profile of your Perfect Job:

1. a) What are you good at?

Everyone is good at something. Many people are good at several things. Think about previous jobs you've had. What skills did you use successfully? Think about your academic history. Which classes did you do well in? What topics and abilities did those classes involve? Think about your hobbies, extracurricular activities, and other groups in which you have been involved *outside of work and academics*. In those areas, what projects have you successfully completed? What skills did you effectively use in those projects?

Along the same lines, everyone is *bad* at some things. Think about what you *aren't* good at, and avoid those things!

Here are some skills to consider:

Public speaking/presentations	Creative writing
Mathematics	Teaching
Training	Counseling
Creating marketing materials	Selling
Creating public relations materials	Corporate strategy
Computer programming/Internet design	Creating artwork
Science and laboratory work	Engineering
Managing people/projects	Research
Problem solving	Crisis resolution
Organizing people/projects	Analysis
Persuasive argument (written, oral)	Editing

Picking your strongest skills will not only bring you closer to identifying your Perfect Job, it will also set you up for success. You will have an easier time landing and succeeding at your Perfect Job if it involves skills you are already good at!

1. b) Of the skills you are good at from 1.a), which ones do you actually *enjoy* doing?

There may be several things you are good at. Which ones do you really enjoy doing? **These are the skills to write in your Perfect Job Profile.** It is not true that all things you are good at you also enjoy. I know many lawyers, doctors, lab workers, and others that are excelling at, or at least doing satisfactory work in, their jobs but do not actually enjoy their work very much. Don't pigeonhole yourself into a career that is based on a talent of yours that you do not particularly like to utilize. Remember, your Perfect Job is not only a job at which you will succeed, but also a job through which you will gain fulfillment and happiness.

2) What topics/industries interest you?

Think about what types of industries you enjoyed studying in school or focusing on in a school project. Think about what topics or companies you enjoy talking about with your friends or family. Even consider what types of magazines and books you like to read and TV shows or films you like to watch. All of this data should point out the fields and/or industries you are naturally drawn to. Write them down in your Perfect Job Profile.

3) What type of coworkers and clients would you like?

Are you most comfortable around your peers? Or are you looking for a lot of mentors? By definition, mentors are more experienced and therefore are typically older than your peers. Do you love to work with the elderly? How about with children?

Think about which demographic groups you most enjoy being around in your personal life. These are probably the types of coworkers and clients you would most enjoy working with, too. Write them down.

4) What size company would you like?

Do you want to work at a large, medium, or small company? The bigger the company, the more coworkers you will meet. Also, the bigger the company, the more types of jobs will be available to you, both as your first job and as future jobs into which you could be promoted or transferred. On the other hand, smaller firms usually offer less bureaucracy and more flexibility. These circumstances would enable you to gain responsibility and grow professionally more rapidly than you would at a large company.

Those are the typical tradeoffs between large and small companies. If you can't decide which one is right for you, consider medium-sized companies. They can offer the best of both worlds.

5) What size city would you like to work in? Is there a specific city you want to work in?

Do you want to work in a large, medium, or small city? A suburb? How about a rural location?

Do you want the opportunity to experience a nightlife after work? Then larger cities are the way to go.

Maybe you want a location that is close to your family? (Or are you trying to move far *away* from them??)

How long a commute can you tolerate? Do you have a car, or will you need a location that is accessible by public transportation? What are the commuting costs? Keeping those answers in mind, which locations are feasible?

Do you have a favorite city? A home city? What about a city you always wanted to live in or at least try out for a few years? Go for it—this is your dream job after all!

Think carefully about these questions and record your answer in your Perfect Job Profile.

6) What hours can you work?

What work hours can you tolerate? Do you want 9 to 5 Monday through Friday, or can you handle overtime? What if the job requires lots of overtime—nights and weekends? What if the job requires working nights or weekends *instead* of weekdays? Be sure to consider the sacrifices in your personal life that long or irregular hours will require.

Do you need a flexible schedule? You may need flex time due to commuting challenges or child care requirements.

7) Do you prefer a client-based or internally focused position?

Do you like working with clients? Or do you only want to interact with coworkers inside your company? Bear in mind that client-based work usually means that the content and flow of your work is dictated by clients, making it less under your company's control and therefore less predictable. In addition, client-based professions place a high value on employees' sales abilities (to bring in new clients and retain existing clients). This is particularly true as employees become more senior within the organization. If acting in a sales capacity as part of your job is a turn-off, think carefully before pursuing a client-based job.

8) How much intellectual challenge do you need?

How much intellectual challenge do you need in your job? There is a wide spectrum of how much true intellectual challenge is offered by different careers. Jobs with little intellectual stimulation can be a rude awakening to those coming out of full-time academic programs. Schools by definition offer nearly nonstop intellectual challenge, yet the real world of jobs offers a disappointingly low amount in many cases.

9) Do you have a salary requirement?

If you know you need to make a certain amount of money, or at least prefer to, then put that in your Profile. If you are okay starting at a low salary but need significant potential for a higher income in the future, put that in your Profile. In order to learn what the minimum after-tax annual income is that you will need to cover your expenses, you may need to create a personal budget. To estimate after-tax income, reduce pretax annual salary by 35%.

I would suggest being as flexible as possible when it comes to salary, particularly if you are trying to break into a new profession or are looking for a job in a bad economy. Although it is true that some jobs pay much more than others, many jobs provide enough income for an acceptable quality of life, and if you stick with it, greater riches should come down the road.

Salary is the last primary question for your Perfect Job Profile because it is truly the least important criterion when you are starting a new career. Don't make a high salary a priority at the beginning of your career; focus instead on the other criteria for your Perfect Job. Once you are established in your Perfect Job, the success you achieve will eventually be appropriately rewarded. Remember, there is no price on happiness; do not be blinded by the pursuit of the almighty dollar at the expense of other, more fulfilling criteria.

10) Miscellaneous Factors

○ **Repetitive job tasks or variety?**

Do you prefer to become an expert at something quickly through repeated tasks? Or do you crave the challenge of a wide and changing set of responsibilities?

○ **Project-based or task-based work?**

Do you seek work that comes as projects? Consider the potential downside of projects that could take months or even years to complete. Instead of projects, would you prefer to handle specific tasks that occur on a regular, perhaps daily, basis? Consider the potential downside if these tasks are only one part of a bigger whole and therefore offer you little exposure to the "big picture."

o   **Structured or open-ended work process?**

How much flexibility do you want for *how* you go about doing your work? Some people are more comfortable when their employer requires one or more specific approaches to completing a job. Other people find that situation very confining and instead prefer to create their own ways of completing their job. Of course, certain jobs have only specific ways to be completed successfully—is that a positive or a negative for you?

o   **Fast-paced or slow-paced job?**

Does the thought of a job where you are constantly under the pressure of deadlines excite you? Or do you prefer a calm workplace without specific deadlines? Some jobs have you "putting out fires" constantly; this can be a source of great stress or great motivation and satisfaction, depending on the type of person that you are.

o   **Receive training or be "thrown into the fire?"**

Some companies offer formal training programs before you actually start working. These can last days, weeks, or even months. Some companies provide no training and place you at your desk working on your very first day on the job (the so-called "thrown into the fire" approach). Are you competent and secure enough in your new job not to need training? If the answer is no, and there is no formal training offered, are you outgoing enough to ask anyone and everyone around you enough questions to figure out how to do your job? Or will there be a mentor firmly in place to guide you and who has the time to do so? Will you instead need to take classes outside of work in order to gain the necessary competency? Are you willing to pay for these classes yourself if they are not company-sponsored?

○ **Promotion-specific or undefined career track?**

Do you seek the structure of a step-by-step path up the corporate ladder? Or can you accept an undefined path to the top? Some companies structure their workplace with positions that have clearly defined rankings. Those that don't will typically require a more aggressive approach on your part for you to be promoted.

○ **Hierarchical or flat organization?**

Some companies have a rigid organizational structure with detailed titles and many layers of staff. Some companies are flat, where everyone is expected to wear many hats and few areas of work are off limits. Which appeals to you?

○ **International or domestic firm?**

Do you wish to work at a global company and interact with people from different countries and cultures and who may speak different languages? Or are you more interested in a U.S.-only business?

o **Travel?**

Are you willing to travel for your job? Most people who travel often for their jobs will tell you that it sounds a lot sexier than it actually is. It can be a solitary experience, and sometimes you are sent to locations you have no interest in visiting. Also, consider the disruption to your personal life that frequently being away from home can cause. Burnout can come quickly. Frequent travelers even miss out on some of the professional relationships that are built by people who are at the office more consistently. Consulting and sales are two careers that typically require a lot of travel.

o **Manager style?**

Do you prefer a hands-on or hands-off manager? Some people want the support and direction of a hands-on manager, others find it suffocating.

o **Work-group style?**

Do you prefer to work independently or as part of a team? If you are part of a team, then you will be partially relying on the quality of other people's work for the success of tasks and projects on which you work. This could be a good or bad thing, depending on the competency of the other members of your team. On the other hand, many people enjoy the camaraderie and support that a close, interdependent work group usually offers.

○ **Organizational culture?**

Companies have their own personalities. Do you like a very professional and serious atmosphere? Or do you like a free-wheeling and very open workplace culture? Some industries lend themselves more readily to one or the other of these extremes. For example, financial services and law are often more conservative and professional, whereas advertising and startup technology are often more laid-back and flexible.

Find Your Perfect Job by Answering One Simple Question

Confused? Are you finding it difficult to decide on answers to even just the first two questions in the previous section? Then take a step back. Here is the quickest way to figure out what your Perfect Job is: **Ask yourself if a job you are considering is something you would do in your free time.** No one is requiring you to do it, you don't get paid for it, you are on your own time and at that moment you can do anything you want to for enjoyment—would you do this job and enjoy it?

If you aren't even sure what types of jobs are out there in order to ask yourself the above question, then take a step further back: Ask yourself what you *do* in your free time. What fields do you find yourself reading about in your spare time? What are your hobbies? **What are you passionate about?** Maybe you love music, animals, drawing, investing, politics, writing, fashion, etc.? Then THAT is most likely the field where you will find your Perfect Job! Go back and complete your Profile, building a *real-world job* around that interest.

This approach really helped me. While I was working as a lawyer and contemplating changing careers, I found myself spending a lot of my free time involved with the stock market: investing in stocks, studying the market, reading books and online articles about investing and the market, etc. Then one day it occurred to me that if I was loving spending my free time doing something that I could get paid to do, then why not pursue an actual job doing it? And that is what I did. In my case, I needed to return to business school to get the advanced financial training necessary to be a professional investor. So I pursued an MBA at a top school (known as especially strong in finance), undertook a rigorous job search, and, after a lot of hard work, landed my Perfect Job as a stock picker for a multibillion-dollar investment fund. This was a substantial career change, yet my natural passion and talent for the job gave me the energy and confidence to take these steps and make the change. My passion and talent also showed through during interviews, helping me land that crucial first opportunity in my new career.

(My story also illustrates that it is never too late to find your Perfect Job and that if you are not in your Perfect Job, it can be corrected.)

Research Real Jobs that Match Your Perfect Job Profile

By answering the questions in this chapter, you created a list of the skills you are good at and enjoy, the fields you are interested in, and the type of company, co-workers, city, hours, client vs. internal focus, intellectual challenge, and salary you ideally want. You also provided additional details through considering the Miscellaneous Factors. Look at the page—it is the Profile of your Perfect Job. What is it telling you? What jobs fit this Profile? **Brainstorm actual jobs that fit your Perfect Job Profile.** Show the list to people you know and ask them what jobs fit this Profile. Ask your friends, relatives, teachers, former bosses, etc. Search the web for job categories and see where there is a match with your Profile. Learn about as many jobs as you can; there are probably many jobs out there that you don't even know exist. (While you are doing all this, be alert for any contacts and/or companies you learn about that would be useful to you once you begin your search for actual job openings, and write them down.)

In order to narrow things down and identify a specific job title, you may find it necessary to conduct **informational interviews** in the industry you've chosen. Informational interviews involve contacting people you may or may not know, but who work in careers you are interested in, and then meeting with them to gain insight into their careers and how they conducted their job searches.

So, find contacts inside the industry (using the methods described in Chapter 4), meet with them for informational interviews (or conduct the interviews over the phone if you can't meet in person), show them your Perfect Job Profile, and ask what job title they think is the closest match. These contacts can also provide invaluable advice on breaking into the industry and should be reached out to again when you begin applying for jobs.

Another way to learn about an industry and different roles within it is to attend meetings, conferences, and/or seminars run by professional organizations in that industry. If these meetings are closed to the public, try contacting the group's leaders and ask if you can attend simply for educational purposes, explaining your career interest in the industry. If you gain admission, learn as much as possible and try to gain contacts for informational interviews or other networking later on.

Attach a Job Title to Your Perfect Job Profile and Focus!

Once you've done all your research, **pick the specific real-world job that best fits your Perfect Job Profile and attach that job title to your Profile.**

Keep in mind that no job will be completely perfect. There are tradeoffs with every choice you make in life, including choosing a dream job. Don't drive yourself crazy going back and forth in your mind between options, trying to reconcile how one job has something you really want and another job doesn't, while the other job has something else you really want that the first one doesn't. Force yourself to prioritize the different parts of your Profile. The stars you used to highlight certain factors when you first created your Profile should help you do this. If it came down to it, and you *had* to choose one factor over another, which would you choose? Force yourself to decide which is more important to you. If you need to, rewrite your Profile by ranking each criterion from number one on down, no ties allowed. Then pick the job option that best fits the ranked criteria to be your Perfect Job.

And remember this: Even if you choose a career option that turns out *not* to be your Perfect Job, you can always renew your job search and pursue the alternatives. Your decision is not irreversible, so give yourself a break. On the other hand, you *must* make a choice at the outset of your search. **One of the keys to a successful job search is being *focused*. Identify your Perfect Job and commit yourself to landing it.** As you go forward in your search, any time the topic of your job search comes up in conversations with anyone, you should say "I want to do <insert Perfect Job title here>," *not* "I don't know what I want" or "I'm applying for X, Y, and Z jobs" (unless those jobs are all very related to each other). Make your job search as specific as possible based on all of the criteria in your Perfect Job Profile—this will make everything you do going forward that much easier.

In my case, before going to business school, I defined my Perfect Job as being an equity research analyst for a buy-side investment firm in Boston. So, while I was *in* business school, I focused all my efforts on pursuing only equity research analyst jobs at buy-side investment firms in Boston. My business school classmates thought I was crazy (or at least unwise) to limit myself this way. But I knew that there is nothing more powerful in undertaking a job search than having a laser focus on an exact job that you know will make you happy. Any efforts spent on other alternatives are efforts that instead could have been directed toward landing your Perfect Job. So all of my efforts were devoted to landing my Perfect Job, and that is what I achieved.

CHAPTER 3

ADDITIONAL CONSIDERATIONS
ABOUT YOUR PERFECT JOB

Still Can't Figure It Out? Don't Panic!

Still having trouble identifying your Perfect Job? Don't get too worried. Many people don't figure out what the right job is for themselves till their late 20s or even their 30s or later. Don't put unnecessary pressure on yourself when you are young and can't seem to find the right fit. Your Perfect Job search can be a process of growth, of getting to know yourself, and of learning what actual jobs are really like (see the next section, The "Chicken or the Egg" Dilemma). Accept your situation, remove the pressure, and just keep learning—you will eventually gravitate toward the best fit.

Hopefully though, your first attempt at completing the Perfect Job Profile has provided you with enough information to get you started in the right general direction. As you learn more over the years, go back and edit your Perfect Job Profile to incorporate what you learn. The Profile of your Perfect Job will become more and more clear.

It is certainly preferable to try new careers while you are young rather than later in life. But pick carefully! Once you start down a career track, it is harder to get into other ones. If you have chosen the right career track but not the right job within that track, you will have an easier time moving into the right job within that track than if you are in the wrong career track altogether and need to change tracks completely to get to the right job.

The "Chicken or the Egg" Dilemma

One of the trickiest parts of a job search is how diffi-cult it is to know what a job is *really* like before you take it. The only way to really know what a job is like is to actually be in the job for a month or more. But we are trying to identify the Perfect Job for you to pursue in the first place, not learn about it after you are already in it! If only you could just go from chair to chair, trying different jobs in different organizations and then make your deci-sion. But you can't do that in the real world.

Some job features are very difficult to know until you are actually in the job. If those things turn out to be wrong for you, it will be too late to change your mind, because you've already committed yourself to the job once you've started working (not to mention you've also invested time finding the job). Some of these hard-to-know-ahead-of-time job features include: What exactly will your typical workday be like? Will your boss be reasonable and attentive to you? Will you like your co-workers? You will probably have spent time with your future boss and coworkers during the interview process, so you will have some feeling for how your relationship with them might be before you accept the job. They probably will also have told you about what your normal day on the job will be like. But interviewers are usually on their best behavior during interviews, not revealing the different sides of themselves. It will be difficult to know what it will *really* be like to work with your boss and coworkers on a daily basis before you are in the job. Also, they often can't, or won't, tell you about the more mundane parts of the job during the interview process. After all, they are trying to fill the position, and it won't help them do that by focusing on the negatives!

Unfortunately, there's no good solution to this. That said, the better you construct your Perfect Job Profile and the more faithful you are in finding a position that closely matches that Profile, the lower the chances are that unpleasant surprises await you at the job. Also, remember that there will always be things out of your control, such as interviewing with one boss you really like and then having him depart one month into your new job and be replaced with a boss who is less compatible with you. Beyond that, do your homework! Ask your friends and acquaintances what the reputation of your potential employer is. See if you can get the inside scoop on how a boss is, perhaps by following up with your future coworkers after you get the job offer and asking them some fairly direct questions about the work environment. This practice is definitely acceptable. Some employers who offered me jobs volunteered on their own to make coworkers available to me for any follow-up questions I had after I received their offer. Remember, they want as good a fit as you do! Finally, if you are still in school, pursue internships in order to "test drive" specific jobs and specific employers. (Internships are detailed later in this chapter.)

A Reality Check for Those of You Dreaming BIG

Be realistic. If you define your Perfect Job to be a job that is extremely hard to land, then no matter what your talents are, you had better think of a Plan B—another job that you would be happy in if Plan A doesn't come through. How many times have we heard the following: A new actress who makes it big in Hollywood or a new band that breaks through to the commercial mainstream is being interviewed, and when asked about their road to success, they say something like this: "I worked hard and stuck to my dreams. Everyone out there should just keep at it and stay true to their dreams and it will happen for them. Look at me!" I actually agree with the gist of that advice. Just please remain realistic. For every actress or band that achieves a successful and lucrative career, there are thousands of other talented and driven actresses and bands that do not make it to the big time.

The point of what those successful actresses and bands are saying is true for hard-to-land corporate jobs and fits perfectly with the premise of this book: Define your Perfect Job and pursue it vigorously and persistently. However, don't let comments from the rare individual who lands a "dream job" mislead you into thinking that everyone who works hard for an extremely hard-to-land job will eventually achieve their big dream. There is no such guarantee. As long as you are aware of the long odds and are still willing to hang in there and go for it, then carry on! But have a Plan B ready that can at least fill the time before you get your big break. Sometimes Plan B isn't so bad itself, and develops into a happy career of its own, replacing Plan A.

A Note for Those Still in College or Graduate School

It's never too early to complete the Perfect Job Profile. Complete the Profile while you are still in an academic program, and it will help you focus on what your professional goals are for after the completion of your program. Even if you are still in the process of figuring out what your skills are, you probably already have ideas for your dream industry. Complete as much of the Profile as you can, and use it to assist you in picking classes, extracurricular activities, and internships that align with that industry and with other job factors you feel confident about at this stage. Edit your Profile as you learn more about yourself and the opportunities that are out there.

Internships deserve specific mention in this process. Internships are an important early step in learning about the real world of work and defining your Perfect Job. Summer or in-school internships are rare opportunities to try out your targeted job and/or employer and see if you like them before having to make a more permanent commitment. Internships also provide crucial work experience and a demonstration of your commitment to a particular career, both of which will greatly strengthen your application for a full-time job in that field in the future. In fact, if the fit is right, successful internships often lead to full-time job offers from the internship employers themselves! So, how do you land an internship? Use the same strategies presented in Chapter 4 about landing your Perfect Job for landing an internship.

The goal of all of this is to get you started on the best professional path for you. Putting in a little extra time before more permanent decisions need to be made will help start you on the right path. In the end, this will save you a lot *more* time later on by avoiding the need to undertake a major career change if you were to head down the wrong path at the outset.

A Note for Those Graduating from College

The transition from college to the real world of work may be difficult for those of you who are graduating seniors. After spending four years surrounded by your peers and living a schedule of your choosing at school, you find yourself in a rigid Monday-through-Friday work week and in an environment filled with people of all ages and backgrounds at the workplace. It can be a shock.

I cannot emphasize enough how important work environment is, particularly when you are undergoing the major life transition from full-time student to full-time worker. Think carefully while filling out your Perfect Job Profile about how you want your work environment populated. For example, in my first full-time job after college, I had no peers for coworkers, and I found that very challenging. I had no peers to relate to and use for support on those inevitable bad days that come with every job. I also had no chance to make new peer friends at my job. This was all happening while the college friends I had around me for the previous four years had splintered away to different parts of the country in pursuit of their own professional goals. I hadn't given enough consideration to the importance of work environment and coworkers, and paid the price. Heed my warning, and pay close attention to choosing your work environment!

The Graduate School Decision

Think about the educational requirements for your Perfect Job. Your Perfect Job might require an advanced degree, such as a Masters, PhD, or JD. If so, you will need to go back to school and get that graduate degree. Another potential scenario is that you lack relevant experience for your Perfect Job and your job search would be greatly facilitated by obtaining an advanced degree, even though it may not be specifically required for the job.

Generally speaking, improving your education is a good thing, both for personal development and for enhancing your career prospects. However, make sure to do a cost-benefit analysis on the time, money, and effort you will spend on graduate school compared with staying in the working world to achieve your professional goals. In doing this comparison, keep in mind that the financial cost of going back to school is not just the money you spend on the education. You also need to factor in the money you are *forgoing* by not working during the time you will be in school. Economists call this the "opportunity cost." For example, let's say tuition, room, board, fees, and living expenses for a two-year graduate program you are considering add up to $100,000. Your total financial cost is actually $100,000 *plus* two years' worth of the after-tax salary you would make at your current job during that time. Compare this total cost with the potential benefits of grad school, such as a quicker path to your Perfect Job.

Of course, you can avoid the opportunity cost by continuing to work and pursuing graduate school part time. Bear in mind, though, that it typically takes longer to complete a program if you only go part time. In addition, many programs are only available full time.

(For those of you interested in law school and/or business school, you can find the inside scoop on those programs in Chapters 5 and 6.)

CHAPTER 4

LAND YOUR PERFECT JOB

It's All about Attitude—Stay Positive, No Matter What!

The process of landing your Perfect Job can be very long and very trying. It is often full of dead ends. You need to stay focused, confident, and optimistic in the face of frequent rejection. You must maintain a positive attitude throughout the process, putting a positive spin on everything and anything that comes your way. You must show enthusiasm to everyone you meet, regardless of whether you are genuinely feeling it at that moment or not. You must be patient and persistent. Needless to say, you must be, or become, someone who takes the initiative.

Make your rock-solid commitment to landing your Perfect Job clear and compelling in all communications during your search. Have an "elevator pitch" ready to go and do not be afraid to bring it up at any opportunity that presents itself. An elevator pitch is a 30- to 60-second summary of what you are looking for and why you would be good at it. Think of a scenario where you are riding in an elevator with the hiring manager for your Perfect Job; what would you say to him or her in the limited time you are together? Avoid clichés and be specific (e.g., include the specific job title of your Perfect Job and your specific relevant strengths).

How to Land Your Perfect Job

Follow these three steps to land your Perfect Job:

1) Identify companies that offer your Perfect Job.

By now you have shown your Perfect Job Profile to many people and undoubtedly have received suggestions on employers. Try Googling the job title and/or company type to get more ideas for potential employers. Try putting the job title and/or company type into Wikipedia.org and see what companies show up.

Make a list of the companies that fit your Perfect Job Profile and are likely to have your Perfect Job position. These will be your **target companies.** Consider creating a simple spreadsheet file on your computer to organize the information you learn about target companies. The sheet would list the names of target companies in the first column, the website addresses of target companies in the second column, and any notes you might want to add about the target companies in the third column. The second column should be hyperlinks, such that you can return to your spreadsheet anytime and click on the links for easy, direct access to the target companies' websites. The third column is useful for keeping a record of communications between you and the target companies as well as specific information you learn about the companies that you want to remember.

2) Find openings for your Perfect Job at your target companies.

At the target companies, find live job openings that match your Perfect Job as closely as possible. These are your **target jobs.** Research the job openings posted on the websites of the target companies listed in Step 1 to find target jobs. Contact those companies directly that don't list their job openings on their websites to inquire about openings.

Search Monster.com, CareerBuilder.com, and HotJobs.com for employers and openings you may have missed. These are the top three websites where employers list open positions, and they are free for applicants to use. You can run searches on those websites for your position and location preferences. (Note: At this writing, Monster is acquiring HotJobs; it is unclear if their respective contents will be merged.)

In your Google search in Step 1 above, you probably found some specific-industry job websites that you should explore. For example, if you Googled a financial services job title, some websites probably appeared that are solely devoted to job listings in the financial services industry. Check these out.

Don't forget to check your school's career website for job postings. Usually these postings are only available to students and alumni, so they may be positions that aren't publicly listed anywhere else. Check your local newspaper and other periodicals' websites for job listings too. Finally, try job-search aggregator websites such as SimplyHired.com and Indeed.com.

3) Apply to the target jobs, and then take two more steps.

Submit your resume and cover letter online to those Perfect Job openings you identified in Step 2. Act fast! You don't know how long the openings have been available. Do your best to get your application in as soon as possible, before the employer hires someone else.

Typically, when you apply online, your resume and cover letter are sent to the target company's human resources department. HR acts as a filter, responsible for choosing the most qualified candidates to present to the hiring manager in the department in which you would be working and rejecting the rest. So, for every Perfect Job opening you find, be sure to take these two additional steps:

○ **Identify the hiring manager for your target job and contact him or her directly about the opening.**

The hiring manager is the person in the business unit you want to join who makes the actual decision on whom to hire. He or she is not in HR. He or she is most likely the person you would report to if you get the job, i.e., your boss.

Finding him or her will take some detective work. However, I can tell you from lots of personal experience that between the Internet, phone calls, and inside contacts, it is very possible to get the name, address, phone number, and email address of the hiring manager. (See the next bullet for information about developing inside contacts to help you with this.)

Send your resume and cover letter directly to the hiring manager via overnight mail or by email. Then follow up with him or her in less than a week with a phone call introducing yourself.

The point of this step is to go around human resources, beating the gatekeeper, which is all that human resources is! Hiring decisions are made by the hiring manager, not HR. In fact, HR often does not understand what the job is that they are screening for and how various backgrounds can be appropriate for the job. Focus your time on contacting the actual hiring manager, not following up with the gatekeeper.

o **Find an inside contact in the company and ask him or her to push your candidacy for the target job.**

It's a known fact that the majority of jobs are filled based on personal knowledge about the winning candidate by a current employee. If no one in the group you want to join knows who you are, change that!

Finding an inside contact is easier than it sounds. Ask all your family, friends, and acquaintances if they know any employees at the company that they could put you in touch with. Search your other networks to find inside contacts. These networks include alumni of your college or grad school, and members of your church or other organizations you may be a part of. Any of these networks could produce an individual who is currently employed by the target company. Another method is to search LinkedIn.com or the company's website for professionals working at the target company.

Once you have identified one or more inside contacts, introduce yourself in a professional manner and request a meeting (or at least a phone call) to speak with them. Explain that you are researching the firm and the position because you are applying to join the company. Mention who referred you, or if no one referred you, then mention how you found their name. If your inside contact is distant from the actual group you are trying to join, ask the contact if he or she could find you a contact who is closer. Some people you contact may not be comfortable helping you or may not have the time. All you can do is keep trying until you find at least one ally willing to be your advocate within the organization.

Having an inside contact can be crucial to landing your Perfect Job and a major advantage over the competition. I secured a number of jobs through finding an inside contact at companies in which I initially knew no one. Typically I reached out to alumni of my college and graduate schools. Once I had introduced myself and made a good impression, the inside contacts were willing to put in a good word for me with the group I was trying to join and/or with HR. Again, hiring managers are much more comfortable extending a job offer to an individual that someone within the organization has vouched for than to a complete stranger. If your inside contact can only contact HR, that can still help, because HR also will be more comfortable putting your resume in the hands of the hiring manager if a knowledgeable employee is backing your candidacy. Without this boost, your resume can easily get lost in the large stack of resumes that the HR person must wade through.

The "Chicken or the Egg" Dilemma, Part 2: Starting a New Career

Breaking into a new career can be very challenging because most employers look for prior experience in the candidates they hire for nearly every job. But how do you get your first experience if every opportunity you find requires prior experience??

The situation is not as bleak as you might think. When you stop and think about it, everyone currently employed in a position was at some point new to their position, right? So that can be you too!

No matter what an employer says its specific requirements are, the fundamental reason behind wanting prior experience is that the employer wants to feel confident you will be competent in performing the job before they actually hire you for it. They also would prefer not to have to expend resources on training you. Therefore, the main way to battle the prior experience dilemma is to reassure the employer that you already *can* do the job. Accomplish this by **doing everything you can think of to build a relevant background.** This includes pursuing relevant internships, classwork or full degree or certificate programs, extracurricular activities, professional groups, and even independent projects you complete in your free time. These will all help your candidacy, even though all but internships aren't actual on-the-job experience. **Put them all on your resume**—there's no rule that says only formal jobs are allowed on resumes. Class work and extracurriculars can be discussed under the Education section of your resume, and professional groups and personal projects can be discussed under an Additional Information section at the bottom of your resume.

I landed my Perfect Job as an equity research analyst (stock picker) at an investment firm even though the job posting required experience and I had no prior direct work experience. However, I had managed my personal stock portfolio on my own time over the previous several years, so I included that fact and the performance data of my portfolio in an Additional Information section on my resume. Also, my coursework and extracurricular activities in business school focused on investment management, so I specified this information in the Education section of my resume. These relevant non-job experiences were discussed in my interviews and definitely facilitated my ability to break into my new career.

Do your best to show your competency in your field of choice in these various ways, and hopefully at least one employer will decide to give you a chance. Remember, all you need is that one chance!

The Resume and Cover Letter—Necessary Evils

There's no way around the need to create an effective resume and cover letter for your job search. I advise you to utilize the many resources you can find in your school's career services office and on the Internet for how to write a resume and cover letter. Review the many available examples. Instead of regurgitating the typical how-to advice on resumes and cover letters that you can easily find at those two sources, I will share with you the important insider tips I learned through all my years of job hunting. Follow these tips when preparing your resume and cover letter:

○ **Tailor the resume and cover letter to fit the Perfect Job you are seeking.** Include and emphasize the experiences, backgrounds, and skills you have that are most relevant to your Perfect Job.

○ For each job experience you detail in your resume and cover letter, **write job achievements instead of job descriptions**. Summarize your successes at the job, quantitatively if possible. This explains what you did on the job while also emphasizing what a quality employee you were (and implicitly will continue to be).

○ **Use bullet points and bolding** throughout the resume for ease of reading. Try to use those in your cover letter too. Whenever possible, begin each bullet with an active verb (e.g., led, developed, designed, marketed, managed, organized, sold, etc.).

o **Keep your resume and cover letter each to a single page.** If you can't do that, then you probably are not focused enough, and your primary selling points will be lost among the other details you have included. Hiring managers do not read resumes and cover letters carefully and will not have the time to review multi-page versions of either. When I was hiring an employee recently, I was dismayed to receive a three-page resume from a qualified candidate. Who has time to read three detailed pages? HR people and hiring managers on average spend only 10–30 seconds per resume, so your main points better shine right through!

o Once you have a draft resume and cover letter, **show them to everyone you can** for their input on content and to check for typos. The final version of your resume and cover letter must be PERFECT—no errors allowed! Have as many sets of eyes as you can check them.

The Dreaded Interview—Ten Tips to Slay the Beast

Nothing strikes fear in the hearts of job seekers more than the interview. For many, this is the most stressful part of the job-search process. Follow these tips to improve your chances for success in your interviews and ease your stress at the same time:

1. First and foremost, **be sure to have succinct answers memorized** *before* **the interview to the following two questions:**

o   **Why are you the best candidate for this job?**

Match your qualifications to what the company is looking for in filling the position. Of course, this first entails finding out exactly what it *is* they are looking for in a candidate. If you have an inside contact, see if he or she can help you understand what employee characteristics/backgrounds the company seeks.

o   **Why do you want to work for this company instead of all the others?**

Understand what makes this company different and special, and be prepared to explain that in your interview. Again, an inside contact can help you answer this.

I can illustrate the importance of this from an interview I had when I was just out of college. I was interviewing for a very lucrative and competitive job, and my only interview of the day was a meeting with the hiring manager for 30 minutes. I sat down in his office and this is what he said to me: "Welcome. I have 30 minutes to speak with you. Why don't you use the time to tell me why you think you are a good candidate for this job?" Yikes! All that was missing was him saying "Go!" at the end of his question/statement. Fortunately, I had thought through the answer to that exact question before the interview, so I was ready. At the time, I probably felt like I was unfairly being put on the spot. But looking back now, I give the interviewer kudos. I mean, this is what it's all about, isn't it? You sitting down and describing why you are qualified and would be a good fit for the company. I'm glad he gave me the opportunity to communicate exactly that, without extraneous questions or information taking up our limited time together and detracting from the main points I hoped to convey. In the end, it enabled me to advance to the next round of interviews at that company.

If you aren't asked these questions directly, be sure to work your answers to them into the interview conversation somewhere during your time with the interviewer. If you somehow aren't able to do that, give a brief "closing statement" at the end of the interview that contains these answers.

2. If possible, **try to find out what the employer asked other candidates in previous interviews for the**

same job. You need every advantage you can get in the interview process, and this is a huge one. Ask former candidates, ask your inside contacts, ask HR, ask *anyone* that might know. Think how much more confident you can feel in an interview if you already know the questions that are coming your way and already have good answers prepared. This isn't cheating—it is simply being better prepared!

3. Before the interview, **practice your answers to the questions** detailed in Tips 1 and 2 above, as well as any other questions you think you are likely to get asked. (See the next section in this chapter for examples of more questions you might get.) Practice your answers in front of a mirror. Practice in front of a video camera, then watch your performance. Do mock interviews with your friends. All of these methods will increase your comfort level and confidence when it is "show time" and you are "on," making you a more impressive candidate. Don't be searching for the right words to express yourself on the spot—have the best answers already prepared!

4. Have questions ready for them. (See the next section for examples.) I cannot overstate the importance of having your own questions for the employer ready to go. It signals that you are a prepared person with a high level of interest in the position and the company—two very important impressions to convey.

Also, you may be surprised to know that an unusually high percentage of interviews are made up entirely of the interviewer asking you what questions you have for them. When you have a series of interviews at one employer scheduled for the same day, oftentimes the interviewers who fall later in the schedule or who are more junior than the hiring manager do not have any questions for you. They figure that you've already been asked and have answered all of the important questions, so they want to provide you with the opportunity to have *your* questions answered. Don't be fooled—these are STILL interviews, even though *you* are the questioner! Don't be caught unprepared when this happens to you; have questions ready. I should also point out that many interviewers dislike interviewing and haven't thought about or don't even know what to ask—another reason behind the phenomenon of you needing to ask questions to fill the time instead of them. Also, you should know that it is acceptable to ask the *same* questions of each interviewer.

5. Go into the interview as knowledgeable as possible about the company and the position. Research both these things beforehand, using the Internet, your network, and your inside contacts as resources. The company's website is obviously a great place to start.

6. Try to speak during the interview as if you have been doing the job for years already. Try to speak with some measure of authority. Gain the confidence to speak this way through the methods detailed in The "Chicken or The Egg" Dilemma, Part 2 section from earlier in this chapter. This is a critical way to consciously (and unconsciously!) reassure the employer of your competence for the position. Obviously, this is partially achieved during your answer to the question of why you are the best candidate for the job; in answering that question, you will undoubtedly detail your relevant experiences and background. If you have physical examples of your relevant work to show them or to leave as copies with them, do so.

7. **"Dress to impress."** Wear a suit. It is always better to be overdressed than underdressed.

8. **Maintain good posture and eye contact during the interview.** Smile. Greet the interviewer with a firm handshake, and depart the same way. All of this body language communicates confidence and professionalism —two critical characteristics that employers want.

9. **Bring extra copies of your resume with you.** You'd be surprised how often interviewers enter the interview without a copy of your resume. In my experiences, this happened countless times. Don't take it personally. Show them how prepared and organized you are—have extra copies available!

10. Follow up immediately after the interview with a short thank-you email to every person you met with. This includes employees in any informal meetings that weren't "official" interviews. Be sure to collect everyone's business cards while you are there so you have their contact info.

When I was recently hiring for a new position, I was floored when less than a third of the candidates I interviewed sent me a thank-you note. I mean, how hard is it to write a few polite sentences in an email and send it off? Will this make or break your candidacy? Probably not. But why take the chance when such a minimal effort can avoid the risk of a bad impression (not to mention it is common courtesy)?

Remain in touch with your inside contacts as you go through the interview process. After an interview, send all your inside contacts at that employer an email updating them on your progress and thanking them once again for their assistance.

Interview Questions for You and for Them

Additional Sample Interview Questions
- What are your strengths?
- What are your weaknesses?
- What is your proudest accomplishment?
- What is your career goal? Where do you see yourself in five years?
- How would you/your friends/your former bosses describe you?
- What classes did you like best and why?

Sample Interview Questions for You to Ask Them
- Could you describe what a typical day on the job would be like for me?
- What would you say are the greatest challenges and the greatest rewards from this job?
- Whom would I report to?
- What is the culture like here?
- How has your experience been with this company?
- How will the hiring process proceed?

Of course, these are all generic questions. You will need to be prepared to answer and ask questions that are specific to the field and the job you are applying for as well. There are many resources available that can provide you with generic and job-specific questions—start with your school's career office and the Internet for this.

Beware: Headhunters!

Headhunters are corporate recruiters contracted by employers to find qualified candidates for job openings. They are of no use to entry-level job seekers. Headhunters only help job candidates with significant, directly relevant experience. This is how they add value to a company's candidate search and earn their pay—by finding candidates with specific experience. It's easy to find candidates with no experience, so companies aren't going to pay someone to do that for them! Don't spend time on headhunters unless you are an experienced candidate.

CHAPTER 5

BUSINESS SCHOOL VS. LAW SCHOOL: AN INSIDER'S PERSPECTIVE

&

ADVICE FOR MBA JOB SEEKERS

Business School and Law School

Your Perfect Job Profile may have pointed you toward a career that requires graduate-level schoolwork for entrance. Or, you may have learned that going to graduate school will enhance your chances of landing your Perfect Job. This chapter and the following one give you an insider's knowledge of the two most popular types of graduate school: business school and law school.

Many college students and young professionals at some point consider attending one or both of these professional schools. I attended law school *and* business school, full time and separately from one another at different leading universities. In the next two sections, I provide you with a concise, direct comparison of the two programs, based on my personal experiences. If these programs interest you and fit the path directed by your Perfect Job Profile, use this chapter and the next to understand the schools better and make an informed decision about whether to pursue these degrees.

How Business School Is Superior to Law School

Overall, I found business school to be superior to law school. Here is a point-by-point comparison of the two programs that explains why:

○ **On a full-time basis, business school is a two-year program; law school is three years.**

This translates into one-third less the time, money, and effort to complete business school compared to law school. Do not underestimate the importance of the additional amount of sacrifice required by law school during the crucial early years of your career.

○ **Business school directly prepares you for a large number of professions, whereas law school directly prepares you for only one—the legal profession.**

Here is a sampling of the careers that business school directly helps you prepare for: management, accounting, marketing, sales, operations, and finance. Here is the complete list of careers that law school directly helps you prepare for: lawyer. Are there lots of possible types of lawyer jobs? Yes. But there are *also* lots of possible types of jobs for *each* of the careers that business school prepares you for.

○ **Business school is international in students and curriculum, whereas law school is populated** mostly by American students and focuses exclusively on American law.

If you are looking for a global network and global career, business school is much more appropriate than law school.

o **Business school admissions takes into account who the individual is, whereas law school admissions focuses only on numbers.**

The business school admissions process includes an in-person interview, a series of personal essays (the top schools require six), a thorough review of your prior work experience (prior work experience is actually required), and your undergraduate academic record and GMAT score. In contrast, for law school admissions, your undergraduate GPA and LSAT score are the only important factors. There is a direct correlation between those two numbers and how highly ranked a law school you will get into. Law schools ask for only one essay, it is generic in substance, there is no interview, and no prior work experience is required.

o **Business school strives for personal development of the students; this does not exist in law school.**

Business school programs emphasize personal and professional development beyond academics. They achieve this by strongly promoting extracurricular activities, leadership, project management, teamwork, ethics, networking, and career development. Law schools devote few resources to any of these things, focusing nearly exclusively on academics.

○ **Business school prepares the student for actual jobs, whereas law school is theoretical.**

If you want your coursework to be solid training for actual jobs, business school is for you. If you prefer to learn the theoretical backdrop to your profession instead, then law school is for you. (This point is explained in detail in the next chapter.)

○ **Business school students have several years of work experience, whereas law school students come straight from undergraduate school or have very little work experience (sometimes a year or two).**

Work experience is very relevant to the business school curriculum, but it is irrelevant for the law school curriculum. Law school is the study of the historical development of case law, so unless you worked in a judge's office for the past 100 years or so, your work experience will not contribute to the law school program.

This difference affects students' overall learning, because a great deal of learning takes place outside the classroom between students. It also affects career development, as students with work experience offer networking opportunities to each other and are resources for information about potential careers and employers. There also is a marked difference in maturity between law students who are fresh out of college with zero real-world experience and business school students whose average age is between 26 and 30 and who have worked in the real world.

o **Business school does not have a required professional licensure exam after graduation; law school does.**

Graduating business school is typically all the academic certification that is needed to embark on your professional career in business. In contrast, law school grads cannot be lawyers until they pass a state bar exam—a test offered twice a year, once at the end of July and once at the end of February. If you do not pass the bar exam, you must wait six months to retake it and then hopefully pass, or else never actually join the profession for which you have sacrificed for three straight years.

o **Business school classes evaluate students in a multitude of ways; law school classes rely entirely on the final exam.**

Your grade in the typical business school class is determined by some combination of a paper, a group project, classroom participation, a midterm exam, and a final exam. Virtually no business school class uses only a final exam. In contrast, the standard law school class relies *solely* on a final exam for your grade. That's right: The final exam represents 100% of your grade! There are no projects, no papers, no midterm exams, and class participation doesn't count. For nearly every law school class, you must master a full semester's worth of material and complete a multihour written exam at the end of the semester, and your grade on that exam is your class grade. Talk about needless pressure! Business school classes have final exams too, and they obviously require mastery of a whole semester's worth of material, but the classes use multiple additional methods to evaluate students over the course of the entire semester.

The lack of a midterm exam in law school classes is particularly jarring. Midterm exams enable students to gauge their comprehension of class material at the critical halfway point of a semester. This allows ample time to improve one's work in the class before the final exam, should that be necessary.

Making matters worse, grades generally matter much more in law school than they do in business school. Legal employers almost always focus exclusively on GPA and law school rank/reputation when making hiring decisions, whereas business employers usually assess a range of factors about the candidate, such as prior work experience and personality fit. This ups the pressure on you to perform well on that law school final exam (your one shot!) even more.

How Law School Is Superior to Business School

You are probably thinking: "Aren't there *some* ways that law school is superior to business school?" Yes. These are the two main ways, and they are both very significant:

○ **Law school will teach you to be a better writer.**

There's no arguing that the challenging reading and writing you undertake during three years of law school will make you a stronger writer.

○ **Law school will greatly enhance your analytical, logical, and persuasive abilities.**

I often tell people that graduating from law school is like putting your brain on steroids. Law school's rigorous intellectual curriculum will undoubtedly make you a much more analytical and logical thinker, as well as able to more persuasively argue your points of view. These are powerful tools to employ in the working world, and in life in general.

Is Business School Necessary?

While it is true that you must go to law school in order to be a lawyer, it is *not* true that you must go to business school to be a business person. In fact, there are many, many successful business people in the world who do not have an MBA. Because of this, many people jump to the wrong conclusion that business school is not an important factor for success in the business world. I used to have this false impression myself. But now that I have gone through an MBA program, I can tell you that an MBA is a very valuable education for success in the business world.

An MBA provides you with a broad tool set of business skills, such as finance, accounting, marketing, entrepreneurship, and operations. These areas of business have specific rules and methods that you need to learn, and few jobs would be able to give you the breadth and depth of experience to learn these on the job to the level you would receive in business school. MBA classes are a combination of case-study (real-world, current examples of problems in the business world and ways to solve them) and traditional textbook learning. Yes, there are many areas in the business world where there is flexibility, where there are multiple ways to effectively complete a project. But in business school you learn the *best* ways (proven in the real world) to successfully and efficiently complete a wide variety of projects.

In addition to the valuable skill set and knowledge you acquire in business school, you also gain an impressive credential for your resume and a community of business school alumni to network with. All of these things together make advancement in the business world significantly more likely than it would be without them. In my case, the MBA provided essential training and transition from my nonbusiness career into my business career.

A Note for Those in Business School: Consulting and Investment Banking Career Paths

Most new graduates from top business schools pursue jobs in either consulting or investment banking. Why? Usually because they haven't taken the time to identify their Perfect Job and this is the path of "least resistance." Few people actually state "I want to be a consultant (or banker) for the rest of my career." It is the path of least resistance for the following reasons:

o Consulting and banking firms recruit heavily in the fall of the second (and final) year of business school, which means that students can be completely done with recruiting at the beginning of their second year if they successfully complete this recruitment juggernaut. Job searching is not fun, so it is definitely desirable to end it quickly if you can. Landing a job early in your second year also provides the security of knowing you have full-time employment after graduation—knowing your two-year educational investment has produced something significant. You are also able to enjoy the rest of your business school experience much more—all the time that would have been spent on recruiting during the remainder of your second academic year can now be spent on travel, partying, and maybe even studying!

o These jobs have a formal recruiting process on campus, making them a much more straightforward route to follow than conducting a search on your own.

o These jobs pay a higher salary than most other options. Starting all-in annual compensation for investment banking and management consulting can be well over $150,000; most other options are tens of thousands of dollars less.

o Perhaps most importantly, these jobs keep many options in play for when the student eventually *does* figure out what his or her Perfect Job is. Consultants and bankers deal with a variety of corporate clients and have a variety of projects assigned to them. Therefore, in these jobs you learn useful industry knowledge and develop marketable skills. They are almost like an extension of business school—a point further brought home by the fact that you typically will have many newly minted MBAs alongside you at these jobs. Many job listings for other types of jobs even specifically state that investment banking or management consulting is preferred prior work experience, knowing MBAs in those roles have gained strong experience.

There are two main problems with following the path of least resistance into consulting or investment banking jobs. First, the student is setting him- or herself up for another job search later on, including figuring out what his or her Perfect Job is. Why not take the time *in business school* to try to figure out what your Perfect Job is, especially when you have so much more discretionary time and resources at your disposal? B-school is also an accepted time of transition for career changers—why make life harder on yourself by career-changing out of consulting or banking down the road when there is a much smoother path available during school and you can avoid this extra step altogether?

Second, many business school grads find they are unhappy working as consultants and bankers. Why? The hours are long, the travel requirements can be arduous, and the work flow is often inconsistent and unpredictable, ranging from down time with nothing to do to weeks on end performing near all-nighters. All of this equates to an unhappy professional life and a lack of a personal life. I simply cannot recommend giving so much of yourself to a non-Perfect Job that you will eventually need to leave. (This of course assumes that your Perfect Job Profile doesn't point you toward consulting or banking in the first place!) **Take the time while you have it during business school to find your Perfect Job, and get started on the correct path right out of the gate.**

(Note: The main advice in this section applies to **undergraduate business majors** too. As seniors, they are similarly recruited by investment banks and consulting firms for entry-level positions after college.)

CHAPTER 6

THINKING ABOUT BEING A LAWYER? GET FULL DISCLOSURE FROM AN INSIDER HERE!

The Realities of a Legal Career

If you've ever spent much time watching legal dramas on television or in the movies or reading legal novels, the image of a lawyer that you undoubtedly have is that of a dashing leading man or woman running trials in the courtroom while wielding substantial power outside the courtroom in both his or her professional and personal lives. From these images, you would imagine that the legal profession is very exciting and very challenging. For years, Hollywood and many authors have made a lot of money romanticizing the lives of lawyers in this way. Unfortunately, the truth couldn't be farther from this fiction. This constant mischaracterization of the legal profession has created an enormous gap between the public's perception of the legal profession and reality.

I wasn't someone who got swept up in the Hollywood fairy tale about what being a lawyer is like, yet the power of these images was undeniable on me and everyone I knew as I made critical personal decisions about pursuing a legal career. Even after I had practiced law for several years and knew the truth firsthand, I was constantly being told by people outside of the profession what an amazing job it must be—such was the power of the images that pop culture had planted! To break the hold of these powerful myths on nearly everyone I spoke with, I needed to share many details about the truth.

In this section, I present those details of the truth about the legal profession. I tackle the primary myths and correct the common misconceptions about law school and practicing law. Not all of the myths out there are the media industry's fault; many are logical conclusions that most people would make about the profession—for instance, that law school prepares you to be a lawyer! Other myths are perpetuated by lawyers themselves. It serves their interests to keep these myths alive. These myths maintain lawyers' elevated place in society by supporting the prestige and imagined power the public attributes to their profession.

I was going to title this chapter "The Dirty Little Secrets of Law School and the Legal Profession," but instead I chose the legal world's own terminology for the title. For certain business transactions, our legal system compels "full disclosure" by the parties to the transaction. This means that both parties must provide each other with the "whole truth" about any matters that should be known regarding the transaction, such that both parties are fully informed about all the consequences of their decision before they decide to do the transaction. So, for those of you considering law school, here is full disclosure on the legal profession—the inside, straight story to help you make a truly educated decision about whether law school and the legal profession are right for you, before you take the plunge. I graduated from a top-20 law school, took and passed two of the most difficult state bar exams in the country (California and Massachusetts), and practiced law for eight years in both large law firms and corporations. Here is what I learned....

The Top 15 Myths about Law School and the Legal Profession

This section corrects the many myths that people believe about the legal profession. In order to expose the truth and shed some light on the unpleasant realities of undertaking a legal career, I am very forthcoming about the negatives. Be assured that not only is this analysis based on my personal experience, all of the information I present has been corroborated through discussions with the many law school classmates and legal colleagues I have known throughout my career. I will leave a discussion of the positives to the law schools' own marketing materials.

Myth 1: If you go to law school, you will get a job as a lawyer.

After all the hard work it takes to get through law school, you would think there would be legal jobs available to you after graduation as your reward. This is one of the cruelest realities that law school students learn too late—there are nowhere near enough junior lawyer jobs out there to employ all the new law grads each year! There are simply too many law schools pumping out new grads every year compared to the number of junior attorney openings available.

According to the Department of Commerce, since 1988 the legal-services industry has grown *less than half* as fast as the broader economy. But while demand for lawyers is growing so much slower than the overall economy, supply of new ones is exploding. According to the American Bar Association, in the 2006–2007 academic year, 43,920 juris doctor degrees were awarded, up from 37,909 in 2001–2002.

The legal profession could learn from the medical profession about how to manage this situation. The medical profession handles entry into its ranks by limiting the number of accredited medical schools. Students that are successful in getting into medical school have a very good chance of securing employment as a doctor after they complete their programs, because supply is matched with demand. This is not the case with law school. Needless to say, this reality creates a very stressful and unpleasantly competitive situation for new law school grads.

Myth 2: Those who *can* get legal jobs after graduating law school will make a high salary.

Although it is true that junior lawyers in the largest law firms earn substantial salaries, only a small minority of lawyers actually work for big law firms. Therefore, most junior lawyers *don't* make high salaries.

On top of that, unlike most professions, legal salaries are not growing. For sole-practitioners (who make up approximately one third of all lawyers in the U.S.), inflation-adjusted average income has been *flat* since the mid-1980s, according to the Internal Revenue Service. A survey of lawyers at firms of 10 lawyers or less in Indiana showed that over the five years 2002–2006, wages for the majority either kept pace with inflation or *dropped* in real terms. Another recent survey found that between 1975 and 1995, Chicago lawyers outside of the top 25% of earners experienced a *drop* in their inflation-adjusted average income. Inflation-adjusted starting salaries for law graduates who work for public-interest firms or the government rose 4% and 8.6%, respectively, from 1994 to 2006, according to the National Association for Law Placement—less than the 11% that median family incomes increased during that same period, according to the Census Bureau. The one exception is in-house lawyers; their salaries grew 14% during the same period. With supply outpacing demand by so much, it's easy to understand why salaries haven't grown and in some cases have shrunk across America for many lawyers.

If you want the truth on employment and salary levels for new law graduates, don't bother with the statistics put out by law schools in their marketing materials and given to the organizations that perform national school rankings. In many cases, statistics on employment and salaries are skewed upward because the surveys conducted by each school receive higher response rates from the most successful students. You see, students that are successful in their job search are more likely to share their employment details than those that aren't. The vaunted *U.S. News & World Report* annual ranking of law schools relies on data provided by the schools, and that data is, in most cases, flawed. For example, in a recent report of its new-grad average salary to the magazine, Tulane University School of Law based its data on a survey that only 24% of its graduates completed, and Tulane admitted that these are likely the most successful job seekers—*not* a statistically valid sample!

Another dirty little secret in all of this is the phenomenon of "contract lawyers." Contract lawyers are young lawyers hired as temporary workers. They are paid hourly, and their pay rate and work level are often merely that of a paralegal. Why hire lawyers on contract? Because most legal work is project-based and this allows the hiring law firm or company to make an employment commitment only for the duration of the project. Why hire lawyers for paralegal work instead of just hiring paralegals? Because they can. There is a perpetual glut of unemployed new law grads who will work as de facto paralegal temps because that's better for them than doing nothing at all. They get to at least *say* they are working for a big law firm. So, another reason that employment data reported by law schools is skewed is because contract lawyers are classified by their alma maters as "full-time employed" grads (and are also often categorized as being employed at big law firms), even though they are temporary, are paid hourly at a less-than-associate rate, and receive no benefits.

The whole situation amounts to a trap. Law students usually take on a large amount of debt to pay for their education, expecting to earn enough after graduation to live comfortably while also paying back the debt. Unfortunately, while legal salaries haven't even kept pace with inflation in many cases, tuition at law schools has increased at *two and one half times* the rate of inflation over the past 20 years. The amount of money most students now borrow for their three-year law degree is staggering. In 2008, graduates of private law schools borrowed an average of $91,506, and graduates of public law schools borrowed an average of $59,324, up over 30% and 27%, respectively, since just 2002, according to the American Bar Association. Many new law grads are understandably disheartened when they realize that not only are there not enough attorney jobs to go around, the jobs do not even pay very well when you take into account the significant school debt obligations most grads have.

Myth 3: Law school prepares you to practice law.

You are required to spend three grueling years in law school before you can sit for the bar exam and get your license to practice law—shouldn't that prepare you to practice law? Isn't law school a "professional" school, geared toward preparing you for a specific profession? Sadly, the answer is no. The standard law school curriculum is three years of classes that focus on the historical development of particular areas of case law. Example classes are torts, criminal law, constitutional law, etc. Every one of these classes follows the same method: The class goes through a case book that is a historical compilation of important cases in the development of that area of law. You are learning how legal theory evolved to make up that area of law as it stands now... and that is the catch! You are learning THEORIES. Although it is important to understand some of the theoretical intricacies of law and how it got to where it is today, this is of limited usefulness in the actual current PRACTICE of law. What is much more relevant is the application of these theories to contemporary client requests and how to produce legal documents that solve client's legal problems. Only appellate attorneys regularly argue the finer points of law and therefore need to delve into the history of the development of the law—and only a very small percentage of lawyers become appellate attorneys! For the vast majority of lawyers, this information is virtually irrelevant for completing client requests.

Take contracts law as an example. In the real world, clients pay lawyers to draft contracts that legally secure the clients' rights and obligations for the matter at hand. Contracts law is a required, year-long class in law school. How many contracts do you think students are required to draft in that class? You would think quite a few, wouldn't you? Unbelievably, the answer is zero. How many contemporary contracts do you think students are at least required to *read* in that class? Yep, the answer is zero again. Cases read by students for contracts class sometimes contain small excerpts from actual contracts, but these are usually very *old* contracts and not even corporate contracts. (Corporate contracts are the type of contract that an associate at a big law firm would typically be involved with, because their clients are corporations, not individuals.) As impossible as it sounds, most law students graduate three years of school without ever having even SEEN a complete contemporary contract, let alone learning how to draft one. Instead, they are equipped only with knowledge of the *history* of contracts law. This history involves legal questions that are mostly settled (some were settled more than 100 years ago!) and therefore extremely unlikely ever to come up as an issue in the actual drafting of a contract in today's working world.

Myth 4: Passing the bar exam is a breeze after getting through law school.

This is another one of the cruel realities of the legal world. You just sacrificed a lot of time, money, and effort to get that vaunted juris doctor degree. Graduation is in May, you are excited to begin your new career and leave behind the student life.... But wait! One more test remains! Oh, and by the way, it occurs at the end of July and requires two more months of intense preparation. You mean the studying isn't over? I can't celebrate my graduation in May? I can't travel or at least relax for a few weeks before starting or looking for work? Most of my summer is toast? You got it! Bar exams are HARD. The passage rate on a recent California bar exam was 33%—that's right, only one out of three students that sat for it passed! The rest had to wait another six to seven months before the next exam was even offered. And you cannot practice law until you pass a bar exam.

Bar exams last two to three days, depending on the state, and typically cover 15 or more areas of law. In contrast, exams you took in law school were two to three hours long and covered *one* area of law. Your law school exams were also open book—what's the point of testing one's memorization skills when in the real world you will have books to refer to when needed? That's a good question for the bar examiners, because bar exams are completely closed book, meaning you need to memorize 15 to 20 areas of law and be ready to sit for two or three days straight writing about them. Yes, many of these areas of law are ones you studied in law school, but most are topics from your first year of law school. How well do you think you will remember topics you studied three years prior? Not well, trust me. This all adds up to the necessity of bar review classes—two months of all-day classes, Monday through Friday, in June and July to prepare you for the bar exam after you graduate. Adding insult to injury, the bar review classes are *not* part of the law school education on which you probably just spent over $100,000. They are instead taught by bar exam preparation companies, totally separate from your law school, and cost several thousand dollars to take.

The exam itself is rather inhumane. I remember in college that if you had three final exams scheduled within a two-day period you could request that one of the exams be rescheduled to another day. It seemed obvious that cramming all the exams together would produce suboptimal performance. This logic is lost on the bar examiners, as the exams are full-day exams for two or three days straight.

Myth 5: The bar exam tests material relevant to practicing law.

With all that extra work, you'd think that the bar exam at least tested real-world legal situations, given that passage is required in order to get your law license, right? This is a screening test, isn't it? Unfortunately, like law school, this test is also not very close to the actual work that lawyers do. It mainly tests the components of various legal causes of actions; for example, the four elements required to successfully make a claim for intentional infliction of emotional distress. Yes, this is more useful than the historical legal theory taught in law school. But what about corporate law, a lucrative type of practice that many law grads aspire to? Doesn't the bar exam include the important real-world fields that make up corporate law, such as mergers and acquisitions, banking, tax, and intellectual property law? Nope. None of those are on any bar exam. You see, the bar exam is completely biased toward the general ("small town") practitioner, whose work typically involves wills, real estate, divorces, and personal injury cases. Planning on going to work at a corporate law firm, or a government agency, or in-house at a company, as many grads do? Then the vast majority of what you need to master for the bar exam is irrelevant to your job.

Myth 6: There is one bar exam for the whole country.

Another cruel reality. Even though people refer to "the" bar exam, in fact there are 51 different bar exams, one for each state plus the District of Columbia! And they are all offered on the same dates, so you must choose which state you intend to practice law in and prepare for that one exam only. What if you end up getting a job in another state? Or what if you start working in the state you got a license in but later transfer jobs to another state, as many young professionals do early in their careers? Sorry, you must take the whole bar exam over again in the new state! Most states don't waive their bar exam requirement unless the lawyer has practiced law for five or more years in another state. Some states, such as Florida and California, *never* waive their bar exam requirements. I remember there were grey-haired attorneys sitting in the exam room with me when I took the California bar exam.... And I thought *my* life sucked!

Myth 7: State bar exams contain a lot of law specific to that state.

Because each state has their own bar exam, state law must vary a lot between states, right? The exams must be different from each other, right? Wrong on both counts! Most state law is extremely similar. State laws differ nowhere near enough from one state to the other that it should be necessary for lawyers to start from scratch in getting licensed in a new state. In fact, one full day of every state's bar exam is the exact same test in *every* state—it is a generic "federal" law test! Why do states sadistically put new resident attorneys through the bar exam gruel all over again then? Because of the lack of legal jobs in each state in comparison to the glut of new lawyers produced nationwide. State bar exams are a tool for states to keep other states' lawyers out and protect that state's jobs for those already licensed in their state. Sad but true.

Myth 8: Lawyers spend much of their time in court leading trials (just like they are portrayed in countless TV shows, movies, and books).

Sorry to burst your bubble. Not only are most lawyers not even litigators (i.e., lawyers that represent parties involved in lawsuits), but of those that *are* litigators, most are not trial attorneys. Litigators spend most of their time *outside* of court, and when they are in court, it is to file lawsuits and make pretrial motions, not run trials. You see, the court system in the U.S. is filled to capacity and has an enormous backlog of cases. The system can't even come close to trying every case that gets filed, so the vast majority are settled by the parties or dismissed by the court before getting to the trial stage. Judges encourage this, and the parties usually are interested in settling as well. By settling, the parties avoid the substantial time and expense of pursuing a case all the way to trial. Settling also assures an agreeable outcome, whereas going to trial carries the significant risk that you could lose and therefore receive nothing while still having to pay all the legal expenses.

Myth 9: Lawyers are interesting people you'd enjoy hanging out with (just like they are portrayed in countless TV shows, movies, and books).

Having spent 11 years of my life in law school, law firms, in-house counsel offices, and government legal offices, I can tell you the common traits that most successful lawyers share: extremely anal, extremely detail-oriented, and extremely hardworking—to the point of having a lack of outside interests and/or personal life. Sound like a fun bunch to grab a drink with? You get the picture. Now imagine having ALL your coworkers and bosses be that type of personality....

Myth 10: Legal work is intellectually challenging.

Law school is definitely one of the most intellectually rigorous academic programs you can undertake. But what about practicing law? Doesn't that continue the intellectual challenge? Nope. You see, the vast majority of legal work is document production. For junior lawyers in particular, this involves filling in blanks in previously prepared documents in order to customize the documents for the matter at hand, entering your bosses' edits (numerous times), proofreading, and copying or managing a print job at a professional copy company. None of these tasks is intellectually challenging. I estimate that on average 90% of the time spent on the job as a lawyer is not intellectually challenging, and 10% is intellectually challenging in the same way that law school was. And I'm being generous. What makes this particularly disappointing is that the 90% nonintellectual time is often made up of tasks that a high school graduate could easily complete. This will make you feel amazingly underutilized given your achievements in getting both a college degree and a law degree. Welcome to the practice of law.

I'll never forget the time that I worked for a D.C. law firm and stayed up most of the night flipping through pages of voluminous government filings at a print shop to ensure that no copy had any smeared or missing pages. This work was deemed necessary to be handled by an associate attorney (me) and a partner, and was billed to the client at our high hourly rates. This was in spite of the fact that a print shop employee or at least a paralegal from the firm surely could have completed this task as accurately as we did, and at a much lower cost to the client. Then there was the time I drafted a letter for a senior attorney in a federal agency, also in D.C. This "drafting" involved writing two short paragraphs requesting a piece of information from another agency. It was a simple request letter, yet my draft was then completely rewritten by the senior attorney (and I had to enter her rewrites). This begs the questions of a) What was the point of me writing the letter in the first place?; and b) Wow, isn't there some work above the level of legal secretary that I could be given? These are just two out of many, many examples I could share with you....

Myth 11: Lawyers are typically busy all the time, especially junior associates in law firms.

Lawyers serve clients. Clients control the flow of work they give their lawyers to do. If the client has no legal work to give, then the lawyer has no work to do. This happens more often than you would think. And there isn't much the lawyer can do about it because, again, he or she does not control the work flow. It gets worse: In a law firm, lawyers are evaluated by how many hours in a year they bill to clients. No work means no billable hours. No billable hours means you are less productive and therefore of less value to the firm. And probably very bored, too. Again, you cannot control this—it is project-oriented work. Junior lawyers get the worst of this. When there *is* work to do, it is the senior lawyers and partners in the firm that assign the work, and so in a dry spell they will keep the work for themselves instead of delegating it. Keep in mind, they are *also* judged on their total billable hours for the year. I remember how odd and counterintuitive it felt to walk the halls of my law firm begging partners for work—a too-frequent occurrence for me and the other associates!

Myth 12: Law firms train and/or mentor young lawyers.

Okay, now that we know that law school and the bar-exam prep class don't teach you how to practice law, you can see that it comes down to learning how to practice law on the job (a more stressful way to do it, by the way). Your legal bosses must realize this, and provide formal training and/or informal mentoring to make up for that, right? Wrong. Senior lawyers do not realize this, as they typically have little business sense (remember, they chose to be lawyers instead of business people in the first place). Even in the business world, it is difficult to find a good manager, someone who understands what a junior employee needs to learn and helps guide him or her for the sake of better productivity. In the field of law, you can completely forget about training or mentoring. Even if a senior legal professional knows this would help, remember that in law firms everyone is judged by billable hours, and hours spent training or mentoring junior lawyers are not billed to clients. So it rarely happens. I won't soon forget those early legal projects I received that were beyond document production (such as drafting a contract!); it was a painful realization that I had little idea how to complete actual real-world legal work, and no one in the firm was going to have the time (or people skills, for that matter) to train me!

Myth 13: Law schools and law firms are interested in who the individual is when making admissions and hiring decisions, respectively.

Nope. Law schools almost exclusively use candidates' undergraduate GPA and LSAT score for admissions decisions. For junior associate positions, law firms almost exclusively use candidates' law school GPA/class rank and law school reputation for hiring decisions. Sorry.

Myth 14: Even if there is competition in law school to get the top grades, you won't have a problem being at or near the top of the class.

Many employers, particularly large law firms, only hire candidates ranked in the top 20% of their graduating law school class. By definition, 8 out of 10 law students are *not* in the top 20%, so they have virtually no chance at landing the big-firm jobs. You say you were always at or near the top of your class in college? Well, guess what? So were all of your law school classmates! The competition you face in law school isn't randomly culled from the streets—they are *all* motivated, bright, high achievers who are *all* working toward being in that top 20%. Unfortunately, the odds are against you—80% won't be in the top 20%, no matter how much they think they deserve it!

Myth 15: Even if you can't get a legal job, your law degree will be useful to enter many nonlegal careers.

Think about it: It is hard to land your first job in a new career even when you have relevant education and/or work experience. Now try landing that nonlegal job with just a legal background. I tried, and learned firsthand the complete lack of interest there is in candidates who are JDs or even practicing lawyers. Are there nonlegal jobs out there where knowing the law would help your performance? Yes. Are there nonlegal jobs out there for which having the analytical and writing training provided in law school would help your performance? Yes. But these two positives are worth much less in the eyes of hiring employers than the multiple positives offered by candidates who have directly relevant education and/or work experience.

Conclusion

It is no secret that there are lots of unhappy lawyers out there. Job satisfaction surveys routinely rank lawyers near the bottom among all careers. Hopefully this chapter helps explain why. Many lawyers end up trapped in the profession, saddled with a lot of debt and therefore lacking the flexibility and/or courage to leave the profession. It is difficult to turn away from something in which you have already made such a huge investment. And it is difficult to leave what could be the only field of employment in which you have any experience and land a job in the unchartered territory of a new profession.

Law school and practicing law are not for everyone, so consider the downsides along with the positives before making the huge commitment and sacrifice necessary to join the profession. Are there people who would be happy as a lawyer? Of course. However, it is a much smaller subset of the population than you would think, as I explained in the previous section. The ultimate decision is yours as to whether you are in that subset or not. If you are still interested in this path but have your concerns, I recommend being a paralegal first and seeing firsthand many of the things I described in this chapter. Or at least try to find a lawyer who will let you "job shadow" him or her for a day, following him or her around and seeing what their typical day is really like. Then you can make a better decision for what is right for you. **Let the real-**

world truths about the legal profession inform your career decision instead of the many myths perpetuated by the media, the law schools, and the legal profession itself!

CHAPTER 7

REPRISE: FINAL ADVICE FOR STARTING YOUR PERFECT JOB

Day One

After you land your Perfect Job and are about to start Day One on the job, consider this: **You only get to make a first impression once.** So, arrive early! Work hard! Be the star! Be the person they won't even *think* of letting go should staff reductions occur—be invaluable! Start your Perfect-Job success story off on the right foot.

Not sure what to wear on that first day? "Dress for success!" It is better to overdress professionally than underdress if you are not sure what the exact dress code is.

Scared you don't know what you are doing while everyone else does? "Fake it till you make it," as they say! Be confident when breaking into a new career, even though most things are brand new to you. Remember, everyone started somewhere at some time not knowing much. Be a sponge, soaking in as much information as you can. Find helpful coworkers and ask lots of questions. You'll be surprised at how quickly you assimilate into your company and are productive at your new job.

Concluding Thoughts

With this book, you have been given the tools to design the Profile of your Perfect Job and then to go out and land it. You've gained an insider's view of business school and law school, and can make a more informed decision whether to attend these programs. **Use the tools and information provided in this book to help you define and achieve your professional dreams.** All that is left to say is:

GOOD LUCK IN YOUR PERFECT JOB!

SOURCES FOR CHAPTER 6

Amir Efrati, "Hard Case: Job Market Wanes for U.S. Lawyers," *The Wall Street Journal*, Sept. 24, 2007

www.abanet.org/legaled/statistics/stats.html, Enrollment and Degrees Awarded

http://new.abanet.org/marketresearch/Pages/StatisticalResources.aspx, American Bar Foundation *Lawyer Statistical Report*

William D. Henderson, Indiana University School of Law—Bloomington, "Financial and Billing Survey of ISBA Lawyers," 2007

John P. Heinz, Robert L. Nelson, Rebecca L. Sandefur, and Edward O. Laumann, *Urban Lawyers: The New Social Structure of the Bar* (Chicago: University of Chicago Press, 2005)

U.S. Census Bureau, "Income, Poverty, and Health Insurance Coverage in the United States: 2008"

www.abanet.org/legaled/statistics/stats.html, Law School Tuition

www.abanet.org/legaled/statistics/stats.html, Average Amount Borrowed